Hawk on a Power Line

Penny,

I hope you enjoy
some of these poems.

Your friend,

RB

Hawk on a Power Line

poems by

Robert M. Wallace

R. M. Wa... (signature)

2015

Louisiana Literature Press

Hammond, Louisiana

Printed in the United States of America

FIRST EDITION, 2015

Cover Image: A. E. Landry

Book Design: Marley Stuart

Author's Photo: Cathy Wallace

Requests for Permission to reproduce material from this work should be sent to:

Louisiana Literature Press
SLU Box 10792
Hammond, LA 70402

ISBN: 978-0-945083-40-5

this for Cathy

CONTENTS

The whole design must hinge on not using anything too big for two men to carry along a narrow hillside pathway.

Architect Fay Jones on designing Thorncrown Chapel

HAWK ON A POWER LINE

And to the Fowl of the Air

Adam had it all wrong
When he named the hawk.
Watching something that beautiful
Soar above me
Means much more
Than four small letters
Without even a long vowel
To make it sing.

Maybe it could've been *thunder*
Or *pain?*
What about *indifference,*
Power, or *praise?*
Think of saying,
Easy and clear
Praise circles a summer field.

Or even something so simple,
So honest like *eye*
With its rising vowel
Which in my heart now means
The hazel iris of curved wings.

GREAT SNOWY OWL

The light and the snow are one.
The sky is gone.

White everywhere,
Bone everything.

My long-tailed Ford truck flies
Across the ice, winging toward a tree.

Is this what deer mice fear:
The quick pluck and the sharp talons

Embedded inside cold brown fur—
Rising now, not knowing where?

BUNTING

We bump over the rutted brown ranch road
Holding the side of Stephen's muddy pick-up.
Cathy should be up in the heated cab
Because she's pregnant, due in fourteen weeks,
But she squats on a yellow plastic bucket
Sliding around like butter in a skillet.

The crisp breeze smells like chickens, and a calf
Thrusts a small head against its mother's udders.
Stephen nods at them, saying, "Bunting—
Reminds the mother to release some milk."
I watch the calf, hooves kicking dirt to dust
Clouds that dissolve into a hot brown diamond.
What little I have learned about sacrifice
I learned by playing baseball in the summer.
But those things seem useless as I study
The floating curve of Cathy's belly.
It makes me feel so clumsy, dark, and exposed
I reach for her shoulder and squeeze it hard
To steady her, and to steady myself.

GUNSHOT HAWK AT THE RAPTOR REHABILITATION CENTER

Its one good wing widens;
Kee—eeee—arr claws through the dim heat;
And I feel a hurt for all it has lost
And know I am nothing like this hawk
Because it wouldn't feel pity for anything
As useless as a wing that someone shot.

GREEK REVIVAL PAVILION

Alderson, West Virginia

Because some surgeon wrongly convinced himself
The blue spring water here
Cured hepatitis and other ailments
He built this beautiful pavilion,
Built it with five marble slabs
And twelve Doric columns.

Sheltered from the heat beneath its ornate roof
I wonder at the beauty of our beliefs,
Especially the elegance of our mistakes;
The lasting impact of wrongheaded ideas;
The abiding pleasure of some faulty premise.

If this is all that's left of my mistakes,
I want to be as misguided as that surgeon,
The marble of my mistaken beliefs
Overgrown with dried brown weeds.
I would gladly be wrong about everything
Only to have some pleasing part of me remain
A hundred years from now
Still in a brown, sunlit field.

STILL THERE

The landscape never even knew
About my wild thoughts
Of heaven and giving,
The pleasure in my simple vision.

The green meadow will still be there
Long after I have passed
With its flowers and heavy stream
And dry brown heat in spring.

It will be exactly as it should be,
Exactly as the welcome rain:
The high wind bending tall grass;
The slow wind chilled with wet air.

NORTH ARROW

After the Death of My Friend, S.M.

My wife likes to look at maps.
So does my father.
And last summer, on our way to the beach,
My youngest daughter
Followed along on a map.
I remember the big blue atlas
Open on her lap,
And her small finger
Tracing our route.
It seems to comfort them—
Knowing how to get some place.

I need some comfort now,
But I can't find it anywhere,
Especially on some map
Because its compass rose
Never changes direction.
I can't find peace in knowing
All the long blue lines,
All the shields filled with white letters,
Every interstate, every highway
Always lead to his passing.

HAWK ON A POWER LINE

He'd seen it
Hunt from there before.

In response to some music
And gliding bodies,
It has come
To a great stillness
Larger than these hills,
A calm
The color of winter fields,
Dusk.

COLD WIND

What is the wind but invisible rain
Falling sideways across the land?
It soaks everything in the winter smell
Of burning wood and chimney smoke.
And sometimes people slip in puddles of cool air
And their pant legs stick to their thighs
As if the material were soaking wet.

But this doesn't happen to the old lady
Gazing through her kitchen window.
Because she seems to be scowling
It's easy to imagine her
Collecting the wind in a rain barrel
And washing her hair in it.
She wants it to smell like soot
Smoldering after a home burns.

COAL SHED ACROSS FROM A COMPANY HOUSE

My wife snapped a picture of it,
The red bricks
Overgrown with green vines,
The cement roof
Grayed and chipped,
And a dark square for shoveling
Coal, in and out.

It was just a throwaway shot, really.
She didn't think of it as artistic
Or particularly beautiful,
But it's the one I look at longest—
The simplicity stunning,
Ample and whole.

CHANGE OF HEART

Yes, thank you, Mr. Douglas
Repeats time and again
To neighbors, second cousins,
And friends upon hearing
How sorry they feel at his loss
Or how pleasant and natural
Sarah looked in her coffin.
Wearing a dark blue dress
His daughter hands him
A paper plate filled with potato
Salad, deviled eggs, and ham.
Tomorrow, I'll mow,
He says to himself,
Studying a still cat
Stalking something
Hiding in the tall grass
Until a thick red-chested robin
Rises, like a sudden thought
Of heaven, in the light
Between leaves on an elm tree.

The Tenth Week

I listen to the traffic on Church Street
Blow into our bedroom,
And lay my hand on Cathy's belly
And smell the sweat that mingles with her perfume.

I think of how our baby's inner ear
Formed during this past week,
How the cochlea, such a tiny shell,
And the stirrup meet.

These thoughts are like those headlights
That whiten Cathy's skin,
That slice into the ceiling and the walls,
That cross, will cross again.

My Love for Her

The world can't hold my daughter close enough
So I swaddle her in a soft blanket
And hold her—sheltered
In the cradle of my chest and arms—

And sing, "When the bough breaks…."
My singing is the constant drip
Of water, forming a stalactite,
Cold and hard and sharp.

My love for her has hollowed out
Some enormous cave inside me.
With a waterfall and thousands of bats
It is deep-set, beautiful but dangerous.

One day, she may get trapped in a tunnel
Or drown in some underground pool.

THERE, WATCHING THE WARBLERS

I vowed to learn what they were—
no bird could be that color,
that bright of a yellow?
Only the black outline of wings
blurred them enough to be visible.

There were two or three
whizzing from bush to dogwood,
grass to bush.
I felt so much pleasure
there, watching these small birds,
so much
joy in the yellow blur.

Only later did I learn
these were warblers
at least they looked like warblers from the picture
but it was hard to tell
because that joyful feeling,
that quick movement
wasn't there now.

It Is a Wonder to Me

At the end of one
Of the hottest June days on record
I first noticed
We live among
The air in a full church.

Down splintered back steps,
Through wildflowers
I felt then
A majestic slowness
And sacrifice;

Felt trapped
Within it
The way I live
Within my body.

Moving more slowly now
I pocketed stones,
A box turtle's shell
And a forest fire.

Secure Amidst a Falling World

Secure amidst a falling world
the memory of running in the woods,
dried leaves igniting
like matches under my canvas Converse,

and hurdling—
stretching the lead leg—
a spider web
spun between two saplings.

It's trapped up there,
like some big juicy June bug
trapped in that spider's web,

wrapped in silk threads,
sticky and still,
a meal.

Through the Darkening, I Felt Grateful

Fueled by something
Safe
And remembered
That eludes understanding

It became possible to believe
What connects me
To the pony,
Three sway-backed horses
And the unearthly white
Stones along the levee.

The low sky
Turned a darker blue
Walking home
Stuck somewhere between
Abandoned, transcendent joy
And the surety
Of an open door.

Cut Flowers

And then the day becomes a glass vase
Toppling from an end table.

This is when my feelings are sharp.
This is when my fingers bleed
The warm red of sunset
From picking up the shards of glass:
Mountain, highway, cloud, and tree.

SUMMER AFTERNOON

In the manner of Federico García Lorca

In the shade of a tree
The air is a window.
Someone threw a rock
Shattering a glass pane.

In the shade of a tree
The heat is a dull
And nicked knife
Cutting stale bread.

No one drinks water
In the shade of a tree.
One must drink pink
Lemonade from a jelly jar.

In the shade of a tree
Time is a root
Sticking through
The hard decisions of dirt.

Go on, try.
Dig it up.

MATISSE IN WASHINGTON

I strike a match in the Crazy Horse
And notice the curve of Cathy's wine glass
Suggests the candor of a woman's belly,
Notice the wine, its color, a light pink blush,
Think of her thighs opening like summer,
A pink rose, the prairie rose,
Blooming in ninety degree heat, beside Route 7.
I reach beneath the table, squeezing her thigh;
David reads "In Dreams Begin Responsibilities;"
And freezing rain falls on yellow cabs
Cruising M Street in search of fares.

STARLINGS

Her black paws sinking in the mud, Tess runs
So fast, the outline of her body blurs:
And just as fast, hundreds of starlings scatter
Into the mist, the flutter of speckled wings
Soaring above me in a chain reaction.

A single body, with a thousand wings,
They land in this brown meadow once again
So unconcerned with Tess, the danger she presents,
I think of actions not involving reason,
The need to group together, strength in numbers.
Remember feeling so alone at sixteen
I landed in the backseat of a stolen Ford,
Headed for Myrtle Beach with seven other boys.
Packed so tight, blunt elbows tossed as jokes,
Our apprehension almost disappeared.

Tess barks, flushing a starling into flight,
A whistling glide, almost touching mud,
And when I stand, observing this, my life
Seems as connected to the meadow as that bird's,
As if my sole desire is landing here,
Hiding among the flock.

LOVE LETTER

Pelicans skim the waves
In a semi-circle like a backwards capital *C*.
Their wings flap and scrawl two *v*'s
Onto the warm ocean air, like a hastily written note.
And their large curved throat pouches,
The fat empty *u*'s of guttural, wait for that moment
When something—a blue fish maybe,
Or a scrap of soggy bread—
Presents itself as a meal
And they scoop it up with their long bills.

THREE VIEWS OF THE RIVER

1

Sometimes the river
And sorrow
Are the same thing.

2

Thrown by the goddess Gray Lake,
The wooden shaft of a spear,
Ancient and demanding,
Soaring over green fields.

3

Long movement,
Wide motion.

It won't stop;
It can't.

The current pushes everything along;
It's fast and always.

Everything is moving
Even the stones.

Everything is forever
Especially the soft sun.

This is a time of abundance
And devotion.

In the dark flowing water
A definition of faith.

BURNING

It's not in those wild flowers near the creek
Or in the undergrowth of small green trees

But in the rough shell of a snapping turtle
Concealed among the dingy rocks
Waiting to trap
Bream in the weeds.

When those large hooked jaws
Close on a fish—
When one life is taken
And one sustained—
The turtle's long neck sticks
Out like a candle wick.

June 1943: My Grandfather Enters World War Two

Your mother, gray
Hair rolled up in curlers,
Must have stood in the heat to snap
This black and white photograph:
Your left arm draping
Father's broad shoulders,
The sailor's cap worn at a cocky angle.
You seem okay with everything,
Trying to be stoic,
But your Father only glances at the camera,
Maybe worried about his son,
Or just always angry.
"Say cheese," your mother shouts
Above a rollicking train
That rolls into the picture
Carrying coal from the fields
Of Boissevain, Virginia.

In His Dragon World

In his dragon world, with its eyes as big as the wrecking balls
Tearing down the tipple at Cox Melvin Mine,
With its wings as large as the parking lot
Around the New River Valley Mall,
With its body as long as the line of salt-stained blue Ford trucks
On Route 20 when a shift ends at Pepsi General Bottlers Inc.,
With its teeth as sharp as the knife
Stuck into some drunk last night at Southern Xposure,
With its boils as big as satellite dishes
Dotting the mountains,
With its mouth belching as much soot
As the smokestacks at the Celco Plant,
With its skat as black and unformed
As the burnt-out Rexall Drugstore,
With its claws as shiny white as the aluminum
Siding on the trailers in Boulder Park,
With its scales as bright and shiny
As neon signs for Napa Auto Parts
And Western Auto Parts on Stafford Drive,
Miners lay on their sides under the coal
With just enough space to square their shoulders,
Picks pounding in the vein like a pulse.

Roots in an Old Valley Bell Milk Jug

1

Dark thoughts, uncontrollable
And deep, pushing down,
Crowding everything else out.

2

Words that we want to speak
Cut off by the heavy tongue
Of thick glass.

3

A weightless feeling, unattached:
No dirt, no rocks,
No sand from which to rise.

SMALL ARK

She came here to the creek
hoping to find
something to follow
and abide by
visible in the wild flowers,
in the thick green grass,

and she heard crying
coming from the rough
shell of a snapping turtle
discovered among the reeds.
The dark brown shell
covered with algae and mud
looked like a basket
woven with tar and grasses.

Thrown

Once I found
Some brown bottle glass
Spread throughout a drawer:

One piece so sharp
And thick
It looked like the tip
Of an ancient spear.

It reminded me of my waking
Vision,
My mother
Ambling through
An empty living room,

Her bandaged hands
Unable to hold me
Or touch my face.

HUNGER

Four Fables

A hawk circled a bright summer field. He saw a field mouse and swooped down on it. But he was too late. The field mouse escaped beneath a tangled bush. The hawk couldn't get anywhere near it. He said to himself, "Don't worry, that mouse has to come out some time. I'll just wait awhile." With this, he settled onto a branch overlooking the undergrowth. He waited and waited and waited some more. The field mouse never showed itself, and eventually, the hawk flew away.

All hidden things do not come into the light.

ॐ

The field mouse slipped into the tangled undergrowth. "It's okay," she told herself. "I'm safe now. That hawk can't get me here." Above her, a snake hung in the darkness. It looked just like one of the branches.

Hiding is not the same as living.

ॐ

The snake slithered through staked green beans. "It's time for a nap," he thought. "I'm full...." Before he finished that thought, a gardener brought a hoe down, just behind his head. It slipped between his scales so quickly, he didn't feel it at all.

Our thoughts hide important things from us.

The gardener tossed the snake's head over a fence. It landed on hard ground, and it bounced twice. Dust spewed into the hot air. It stopped on an open brown space between two tufts of grass. Ants swarmed the head, and in a few minutes, it was completely black.

We cannot hide in hard places.

A STACK OF BRICKS

The color of fire—
A flickering red, with some orange
And yellow hidden within the flame—

Burning in the soft blue morning,
Burning in the afternoon blue
And in the heavy blue night.

Burning, just as I am

To become a wall
Or a tall red chimney,

Something necessary,
Something needed.

A walk to the house.

AVAILABLE BEAUTY

This painting by Mark Rothko was a surprise.
When I first saw it, I was tired, waiting
In my wife's busy office. I noticed the card
With "Untitled 1957" reproduced on it
Stuck on a cluttered cork board, almost hidden.
The painting is so very clean and simple:
Two green rectangles, one small and one bigger,
Separated by a thin blue rectangle.
There is something beautiful in the colors,
Something so peaceful in the basic shapes
The longer I studied that stark simplicity,
The deeper that dappled green seemed to me,
The slower that blue rectangle became,
Suggesting an available beauty,
Splendor even in my tangled life.

The painting overwhelms me, makes me small,
And then it makes me part of something
Colossal, beauty and its peacefulness.
I tried to surf one time, to ride the waves.
What I recall most is a tired feeling.
I couldn't pop up on the swaying board;
My legs weren't strong enough for me to stand.
But as I lay flat on the rocking water,
Holding the slick surfboard with all my strength,
Catching my breath from yet another fall,
I felt myself rising within the green,
Even higher within the blue.

SUNDOWN

I want to be here now
With light from the kitchen windows
Disappearing a few steps from the porch
Because this beauty makes me feel
Both loss and wonder, hurt and amazed.

The closest clouds are black
Almost as black as smoke
But further back the clouds are pink
And orange like cotton candy
Bought at a county fair.

Behind the clouds the sky is green,
The same green as the winter ocean
And when I look lower, the sky
Is lighter, the more welcomed blue
Of a warm spring afternoon.

Suddenly only a small strip
Of blue is still visible.
It looks like sediment in water
Settling to the bottom,
Slowly, without any restraint.

THE VENDEMMIA, THE GRAPE HARVEST

Even broken bits of marble
Work themselves into men.

This is the mosaic lesson
Where small pieces of stone become real

Legs lifting, and then falling:
Falling to lift; lifting to fall.

Here forever it's always a beautiful afternoon
And the marble men are always working

And never tire in the abiding heat,
In the Roman sunlight.

Men made of marble
And other bits of stone

Stomp the harvest of full sweet grapes
Into the immense joy of wine.

REDNECK VARIATIONS ON A THEME BY WALLACE STEVENS

> *I placed a jar in Tennessee....*
> —From *"Anecdote of a Jar"*

1

I placed a satellite dish on a roof.
It made the heavenly sky
Disappear into a large gray hole.

2

I placed a speedboat in a river.
The water sped past like asphalt
And sped around, no longer wet.

3

I placed a car on some cinderblocks.
It took dominion of the yard.
The chassis was silver and empty.

4

I placed a house in a fire.
It became hot and red
Like everything else in the blaze.

AFTERSHOCKS

Maybe the janitor just forgot
To unlock
The classroom door?

Or maybe
He lost his keys?

That big key ring
Might have disappeared
Between some seat cushions
In a soft parlor couch?

Or in the red pleather cushions
At the strip club
Especially when Sugar dances
Or when Starlight dances
Or when May Belle
Struts across the stage?

When May Belle shakes
Her hips like an earthquake
Things tend to break
And things tend to disappear
In the wreckage:
Money, keys
And any thought
Of clean floors
And open doors.

FAT IN A PAN

Snow and trees hide the warmth.
Think, for example, of a covered pot—
Water boiling beneath its lid.

If someone lifted the lid, and looked inside,
The water would sink and slow.

It's okay to think of it as slowing,
                                    as dissipating,
But if I touched it, my fingertips would still burn.

The pain could be described as cold.
It is still nothing more than burning.

Frozen dirt and brittle brown leaves
Disappear beneath the white.

When I walk in the winter woods,
Shadows make the snow seem dark
Gray like a skillet bottom.

Even when I tiptoe across
The ice and leaves pop.

WAITING

Under the grackle's words, under the hard bead
Of the crow's eyes, the foal is dropped, the furrow plowed.
—*James Still,* The Wolfpen Poems

The crow's smooth black beak
Curves slowly like space;
Its black claws grasp
The faded gray fence post.

A few feathers just below its wing
Seem blue, almost
But most are dull black
Like a shadow hiding something.

No, more like a dull black piece
Of coal, a chipped shard
Formed from something prehistoric,
Something ancient and creeping.

FIVE FRAGMENTS WITH COLOR

1

The bricks seem to glow,
A soft, iridescent yellow:
In some places, darker, more brown;
In others, lighter, almost white.

2

Sometimes watching the green
Leaves and high branches
Everything curves
And soars.

3

Late afternoon sunlight
Colors the kitchen window
White,
An intense spreading white.

4

The fence is rusted orange
And shadows from the tree limbs
Fall across the chain link in swaying lines
Which makes the rust appear
Darker, heavier.

5

Cold marble
The color of moonlight on night water
Lilies, six soft white petals
Infused with pale blues.

DUMB THING

The creek had risen too high
And I was a fool for trying to cross
The flooded railroad tracks.
My car slid a few feet to the left
Then a few more in the high water.

Gravel scraped the car's steel bottom.
The heavy sound made me mad,
Made me grip the wheel even harder.
The rough noise sounded like stupidity,
Unrelenting, everlasting stupidity.

The External World Is Fitted to the Mind

The external world is fitted to the mind
When sparrows sing
Improvising spring.

Those birds may be our best
Thoughts, foraging for twigs
To build a nest.

But others aren't as useful:
That woodpecker
Pecking the tin roof
                    waking us up;
Or some small finch
Squeezing through a hole
In the attic—panicky
Now—flying into a rafter.

Sunlight on the River

It shines just above the surface:
The beauty of water, the beauty of light.

A whiteness which is almost yellow,
Jagged, and glittering,
Sunlight shimmers over the swell.

It shines, and I want to be the shining
Water in the flashing current.

Viewing My Grandmother's Body

I hear you telling me how
My great grandfather, John Crosby,
Stood in line at Ellis Island
Clutching a single gold coin
His father in Scotland gave him
Before the ship sailed.
                              Now I wonder,
Maybe death is like that: coming
To a new country with no money
Or with a shiny piece of gold?
I want to know what the soul,
Worm and flower, will discover.

ON LOOKING AT HENRI MATISSE'S *WOMAN WITH POMEGRANATES AND AMPHORA* IN THE NATIONAL GALLERY

Perhaps beauty is
A small mistake,
Something sharp and strong;
A devastating
Need to get out
That never heals;
Another thing for the body
To love?

Perhaps beauty is
A clear night
Softer than the fullness
Of a woman's breast?

It is not heavy—
This making myself vulnerable—
But it is large
And unchanging.
It is my secret
The way waves
Will always
Fly like mourning doves.

Perhaps beauty is
The bright lights of a café,
The intoxicating
And deceptive lights,
Rising in every curve
Of her various enthusiasms?

Autumn in Dolly Sods, West Virginia

This in praise of destruction,
Its intimidating joyfulness,
Praise for the ecstasy
Of annihilation,
The elemental quality within
An explosion of green darners:

Late summer storms
Of dragonflies
Hovering above the grass
In meadows and fields,
A darkened sky
Designed for biting and chewing
Preying on clouds
Of mosquitoes and midges.

THE PEREGRINE FALCON

At Overton Park Zoo, Memphis

If we all feed on some violent hunger,
Then this fat gutted rat, gray belly knifed
From throat to tail, has been sacrificed
On a concrete floor that seems to me an altar.

Swallowed by courtly mansion after mansion,
Where servants change the sheets on every bed,
The zoo seems as misplaced as an injured falcon
Eating a rat some worker killed.

Those seconds when I squeeze the iron rail
And imagine its wings pulled back like a trigger
And the diving falcon shot into a roll
And squawks that rifle through the August heat
And the whap sound, an explosion of duck feathers,
Reveal pointed wings in me and a notched beak.

In the Serpent-Handling Church

She took out a two-and-a-half foot long canebrake
rattlesnake and held it up.
　　　　　—*Dennis Covington,* Salvation on Sand Mountain

Since the darkness is always with her
Even when she picks blackberries,
She reaches into the snake box
For the one spirit, the one god.

Transcendence is loss:
Loss of place; loss of self;
No church, no words—
Have your way, Lord.

Handling the snake is a giving in,
A surrender to the twisting darkness,
The cold darkness now within her grasp.

She Tells about the Johnstown Flood

The great flood of Friday, May 31, 1889
killed 2,209, nearly three times the toll of
the great San Francisco earthquake in 1906.
—*From* Smithsonian

We lost everything downstairs—our new stove
we still owed eleven dollars on,
the piano I'd just learned how to play.
My mama swore that we were all fortunate
when I complained about the things we lost.
She said I ought to think of how the Haleys,
who sat in a pew with us at St. Mark's,
lost three out of seven children in the flood
when their old frame house split into kindling.
She said I could've been their youngest girl,
Sarah, sinking beneath the rising water
like a little stone thrown in Conemaugh Lake.
They found her body off of Locust Street
across from the Eureka Skating Rink
impaled on Tommy Logan's picket fence.
When Mama let that slip, I started crying.
I wished that all the rain had turned to snow.
I thought that if it was just January,
then snow would fall, and I would be right there
with Sarah skating over a mirror.

I asked my mama, Why did Sarah drown?
Her answer was the forty-sixth Psalm—
"God is our refuge and strength," Mama sighed,
and I believed her at the age of nine.

But now I know God did not kill poor Sarah.
As I sit here and listen to the rain
and to my own girl playing jacks, I know
our misery was the work of man.
And Daddy knew. He knew the truth of it
while we was sitting on a rafter in our attic
watching the water rise. He cursed Mellon,
Carnegie, and the South Fork Fishing Club
for building a dam with hay and spruce boughs.

WOMAN WHISPERING

Raindrops glaze the windshield.
I glance at the river,
At the mystery of muddy water,
Secret, hidden.

It's almost as though I've just seen
A woman whispering,
A beautiful woman.
What is she saying?
Even if I could hear her
I wouldn't understand
Because she's speaking in the dark
Language of rain.

BEAUTY IS ALWAYS

This pond seems fairly shallow.
Light should penetrate to its bottom

But dark green algae,
A thin layer of scum,

Makes the still water seem solid
Like a dark window pane.

Beauty is always an exception:
A large koi suddenly appears—

A deep and slightly brownish gold
Breaking through murky green—

Then disappears
Beneath algae and weeds.

SWEET SUE

A wrecked sternwheeler rotting on the river,
The sure decay of all our steady travels:

Cold, muddy water moves around and through
The large unmoving paddlewheel;

Elongated willow leaves press against
Busted windows along the upper deck,

And the whole thing makes me think
Of a big dog I saw once on the bank,

Powerful jaws crushing a rat's black throat.
That stray dog shook the lifeless rat viciously

And would not let loose of the dead body.
It wouldn't stop. More likely, it couldn't.

SHIMMER

Streetlamps beside the river
Flicker across dark water:

An open window with white curtains
Billowing into the bedroom
Then receding with the breeze;

The smell of honeysuckle
Sweet but brief
Somewhere along the road;

Icy branches wavering
In the slow winter wind;

A man's fingertip tracing
The deep line of his wife's spine;

A white candle in a drawer
Hidden in shadows.

The wax is cool when touched.

Acknowledgments

The author is grateful to the editors and publishers of the following publications, where some of the poems collected here originally appeared, sometimes in different forms: *ABZ: A Poetry Magazine*; *The Bluestone Review*; *Cold Mountain Review*; *Georgetown Review*; *Inch*; *Kentucky Poetry Review*; *Kestrel*; *Louisiana Literature*; *North Carolina Literary Review Online*; *Now & Then: The Appalachian Magazine*; *Roanoke Review*; *Slant*; *Weeping with Those Who Weep: An Anthology of Poems on Bereavement*; and *Yarrow*.

Author's Note

I want to thank Jack Bedell and his staff at Louisiana Literature Press for helping to make this happen. I also want to thank my teacher and friend, Heather Ross Miller, for her support all these many years.